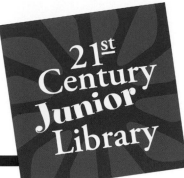

21st
Century
Junior
Library

FARM ANIMALS
LLAMAS

by Katie Marsico

CHERRY LAKE PUBLISHING * ANN ARBOR, MICHIGAN

Published in the United States of America by Cherry Lake Publishing
Ann Arbor, Michigan
www.cherrylakepublishing.com

Content Adviser: Laura Keller, Yellow Wood Llamas
Reading Adviser: Cecilia Minden-Cupp, PhD, Literacy Consultant

Photo Credits: Cover, ©Suerolopez/Dreamstime.com, ©James R T Bossert/Shutterstock, Inc.,
©jadimages/Shutterstock, Inc.; cover and pages 4, 6, 8, 10, 12, 14, 16, ©Laura Keller/Yellow
Wood Llamas; page 18, ©Paula Fisher/Dreamstime.com; page 20, ©photolibrary, all rights reserved

LIBRARY OF CONGRESS CATALOGING-IN-PUBLICATION DATA
Marsico, Katie, 1980–
  Farm animals. Llamas/by Katie Marsico.
      p. cm.—(21st century junior library)
  Includes bibliographical references and index.
  ISBN-13: 978-1-60279-977-6 (lib. bdg.)
  ISBN-10: 1-60279-977-6 (lib. bdg.)
  1. Llamas—Juvenile literature. 2. Llama farms—Juvenile literature. I. Title.
  SF401.L6M375 2011
  636.2'966—dc22   2010030096

*Cherry Lake Publishing would like to acknowledge the work of
The Partnership for 21st Century Skills.
Please visit www.21stcenturyskills.org for more information.*

Printed in the United States of America
Corporate Graphics Inc.
January 2011
CLSP08

CONTENTS

Have you ever seen a llama?

Not Quite a Camel

Have you ever visited a farm? Did you see an animal that looked like a camel? You might have been looking at a llama! Llamas and camels are related, but they are two different animals.

A llama's long, soft hair makes good yarn.

Farmers often raise llamas for their **fiber**. It can be used to make yarn and rope. Are you ready to learn about llamas?

Make a Guess!

What do people make with yarn made from llama fiber? Write down 2 guesses. Then turn to page 15 for some answers.

Llamas like to be with other llamas.

Let's Look at a Herd!

How many llamas live on a llama farm? It depends on the size of the farm. Most farmers keep more than one llama. This is because llamas like to be in groups called **herds**.

Crias can stand up and walk soon after they are born.

Baby llamas are called **crias**. A cria's father is called a **sire**. A cria's mother is called a **dam**. Llamas are adults when they are between 2 and 3 years old. They usually live for 20 to 25 years.

Look!

Have you ever seen a llama up close? They weigh between 250 and 450 pounds (113 and 204 kilograms). They can be more than 6 feet (2 meters) tall. Their fur can be black or brown. It can also be gray, red, or white. Some llamas have spots!

Llamas need room to graze.

Life on a Llama Farm

Most llama farms have a shed or barn. This building provides **shelter** for the animals. There are also grassy fields where llamas can **graze**. Farmers make sure the llamas have fresh water and food. Llamas like to eat hay and grains.

Llama fiber can be spun into thread or yarn.

Many people raise llamas for their fiber. Farmers collect the llamas' hair once a year. This is done by **shearing** or brushing the animals. Llama fiber needs to be cleaned and untangled. Then it can be made into yarn or rope. People use llama fiber to make clothes. It can also be used to make rugs and blankets.

Think!

Do you think anyone besides farmers looks after llamas? Who helps keep your family pets healthy? **Veterinarians** help care for family pets. They also treat farm animals such as llamas!

Some llamas are hard workers!

More Reasons to Raise Llamas

Llamas do more than give us fiber. Some work as **pack animals**. They carry heavy loads for people. Other llamas are trained to pull carts.

Llamas and goats can live together on farms.

Farmers sometimes use llamas to protect their sheep and goats. Llamas are good guards against coyotes!

Llamas also can be used as **therapy animals**. Special trainers bring them to hospitals to visit people. Llamas are friendly. They help cheer up patients who are sick or sad.

Would you like to raise a llama someday?

Llamas even make great pets. Some people show off their pet llamas at fairs. What would your friends say if you told them you had a pet llama?

Ask Questions!

Do you want to know more about llamas? Ask your parents or teachers if there are any llama farms in your area. You can write a letter to the farm owners with your questions. Maybe you can even visit them in person!

GLOSSARY

crias (CREE-uhz) baby llamas

dam (DAM) a cria's mother

fiber (FYE-buhr) thin threads of animal hair

graze (GRAYZ) to feed in a grassy area such as a meadow

herds (HERDZ) groups of animals such as llamas

pack animals (PAK AN-uh-muhlz) animals used to carry heavy loads

shearing (SHEER-ing) the act of cutting hair

shelter (SHEL-tur) protection from bad weather

sire (SYUHR) a cria's father

therapy animals (THER-uh-pee AN-uh-muhlz) animals used to help someone who is not well heal or feel better

veterinarians (vet-ur-uh-NAYR-ee-uhnz) doctors who treat animals

FIND OUT MORE

BOOKS

Hudak, Heather C. *Llamas*. New York: Weigl Publishers, 2007.

Stockland, Patricia M., and Todd Ouren (illustrator). *In the Llama Yard*. Edina, MN: Magic Wagon, 2010.

WEB SITES

DesertUSA: Llama
www.desertusa.com/animals/llama.html
Read more interesting facts about llamas and how people use them.

National Wildlife Federation: All About Llamas
www.nwf.org/Kids/Ranger-Rick/Animals/Mammals/All-About-Llamas.aspx
Learn more about llamas as both farm animals and pets.

INDEX

ABOUT THE AUTHOR

Katie Marsico has written more than 60 books for young readers. She dedicates this book to her "nieces"—Isabella and Emma—in the hopes that their parents will one day buy them a llama.